nickelodeon

TEENAGE MUTANT NINJA TURTLES™

MAD LIBS®

concept created by Roger Price & Leonard Stern

JANPS

PSS!
PRICE STERN SLOAN
An Imprint of Penguin Group (USA) LLC

PRICE STERN SLOAN
Published by the Penguin Group
Penguin Group (USA) LLC, 375 Hudson Street, New York, New York 10014, USA

USA | Canada | UK | Ireland | Australia | New Zealand | India | South Africa | China

penguin.com
A Penguin Random House Company

Mad Libs format copyright © 2014 by Price Stern Sloan,
an imprint of Penguin Group (USA) LLC. All rights reserved.

Published by Price Stern Sloan,
a division of Penguin Young Readers Group,
345 Hudson Street, New York, New York 10014.
Printed in the USA.

Based on characters by Peter Laird and Kevin Eastman.

ISBN 978-0-8431-8235-4
3 5 7 9 10 8 6 4

MAD LIBS
INSTRUCTIONS

MAD LIBS® is a game for people who don't like games!
It can be played by one, two, three, four, or forty.

• RIDICULOUSLY SIMPLE DIRECTIONS

In this tablet you will find stories containing blank spaces where words
are left out. One player, the READER, selects one of these stories. The
READER does not tell anyone what the story is about. Instead, he/she asks
the other players, the WRITERS, to give him/her words. These words are
used to fill in the blank spaces in the story.

• TO PLAY

The READER asks each WRITER in turn to call out a word—an adjective or
a noun or whatever the space calls for—and uses them to fill in the blank
spaces in the story. The result is a MAD LIBS® game.

When the READER then reads the completed MAD LIBS® game to the other
players, they will discover that they have written a story that is fantastic,
screamingly funny, shocking, silly, crazy, or just plain dumb—depending
upon which words each WRITER called out.

• EXAMPLE (*Before* and *After*)

" _____We want 20$_____ !" he said _____QUICKLY_____
      EXCLAMATION   ADVERB

as he jumped into his convertible _____box_____ and
                     NOUN

drove off with his _____SWtdxx_____ wife.
            ADJECTIVE

" _____*Ouch*_____ !" he said _____*stupidly*_____
      EXCLAMATION   ADVERB

as he jumped into his convertible _____*cat*_____ and
                     NOUN

drove off with his _____*brave*_____ wife.
            ADJECTIVE

MA⊙LI S
QUICK REVIEW

In case you have forgotten what adjectives, adverbs, nouns, and verbs are, here is a quick review:

An ADJECTIVE describes something or somebody. *Lumpy, soft, ugly, messy,* and *short* are adjectives.

An ADVERB tells how something is done. It modifies a verb and usually ends in "ly." *Modestly, stupidly, greedily,* and *carefully* are adverbs.

A NOUN is the name of a person, place, or thing. *Sidewalk, umbrella, bridle, bathtub,* and *nose* are nouns.

A VERB is an action word. *Run, pitch, jump,* and *swim* are verbs. Put the verbs in past tense if the directions say PAST TENSE. *Ran, pitched, jumped,* and *swam* are verbs in the past tense.

When we ask for A PLACE, we mean any sort of place: a country or city (*Spain, Cleveland*) or a room (*bathroom, kitchen*).

An EXCLAMATION or SILLY WORD is any sort of funny sound, gasp, grunt, or outcry, like *Wow!, Ouch!, Whomp!, Ick!,* and *Gadzooks!*

When we ask for specific words, like a NUMBER, a COLOR, an ANIMAL, or a PART OF THE BODY, we mean a word that is one of those things, like *seven, blue, horse,* or *head.*

When we ask for a PLURAL, it means more than one. For example, *cat* pluralized is *cats.*

MAD LIBS® is fun to play with friends, but you can also play it by yourself! To begin with, DO NOT look at the story on the page below. Fill in the blanks on this page with the words called for. Then, using the words you have selected, fill in the blank spaces in the story.

Now you've created your own hilarious MAD LIBS® game!

ORIGINS OF THE TURTLES

NOUN _____

ADJECTIVE _____

PART OF THE BODY (PLURAL) _____

NOUN _____

ADJECTIVE _____

ANIMAL _____

PLURAL NOUN _____

NOUN _____

ADJECTIVE _____

ANIMAL (PLURAL) _____

MAD LIBS
ORIGINS OF THE TURTLES

Ninja master Hamato Yoshi was walking home from the pet store,

carrying a glass _____ with four baby turtles when he passed
                        NOUN

a/an _____ man on the street and decided to follow him to an
            ADJECTIVE

alleyway. In the alley stood two mysterious men with glowing

_____. One of the men carried a/an _____
PART OF THE BODY (PLURAL)   NOUN

containing a green slime known as mutagen. Suddenly, a rat skittered

across the alley, and the men in suits lunged for Hamato Yoshi. In

the scuffle, the container of mutagen fell to the ground and broke.

Hamato's turtles fell and landed in the _____ ooze.
                                              ADJECTIVE

Then Hamato Yoshi transformed into Splinter, a rat the size of a/an

_____ and his petshop turtles transformed into human-size
        ANIMAL

turtles! There's Leonardo, the leader; Donatello, who is smart and good

at inventing _____; Raphael, who has lots of attitude; and
                PLURAL NOUN

Michelangelo, who knows how to party like a/an _____.
                                                        NOUN

Together, these four _____ warriors are the Teenage Mutant
                            ADJECTIVE

Ninja _____!
        ANIMAL (PLURAL)

MAD LIBS® is fun to play with friends, but you can also play it by yourself! To begin with, DO NOT look at the story on the page below. Fill in the blanks on this page with the words called for. Then, using the words you have selected, fill in the blank spaces in the story.

Now you've created your own hilarious MAD LIBS® game!

LIFE IN THE SEWERS

ADJECTIVE _____

PLURAL NOUN _____

ADJECTIVE _____

VERB _____

NOUN _____

PLURAL NOUN _____

NUMBER _____

NOUN _____

ADJECTIVE _____

ADJECTIVE _____

PART OF THE BODY (PLURAL) _____

PLURAL NOUN _____

MAD LIBS
LIFE IN THE SEWERS

The Teenage Mutant Ninja Turtles have a/an ___happy___ hideout
ADJECTIVE

in the sewers under New York City. In their hideout they each have a

bed that accommodates the hard, bulky ___candys___ on their
PLURAL NOUN

backs. In the mornings they enjoy a breakfast of ___smellir___ green
ADJECTIVE

algae. Next to the kitchen is the dojo, where the boys can ___shoot___
VERB

and Master Splinter teaches them the ___shark___ of the ninja.
NOUN

After training, it's time to relax. Leonardo enjoys his favorite science-

fiction TV show *Space ___strawg___*! Donatello plays with his
PLURAL NOUN

inventions. Raphael blows off some steam with ___44___ games of
NUMBER

pinball. Michelangelo rides his skateboard through the sewer tunnels

as fast as a speeding ___period___. At the end of a/an ___ridicula___
NOUN   ADJECTIVE

day, the turtles fork down another ___brick___ pile of algae before
ADJECTIVE

heading to bed. But as Splinter turns off the lights, and the Turtles

close their ___legs___, they can't help but wonder if
PART OF THE BODY (PLURAL)

there isn't a bigger world up on the surface, and what ___shifer___
PLURAL NOUN

they might find there.

MAD LIBS® is fun to play with friends, but you can also play it by yourself! To begin with, DO NOT look at the story on the page below. Fill in the blanks on this page with the words called for. Then, using the words you have selected, fill in the blank spaces in the story.

Now you've created your own hilarious MAD LIBS® game!

VISITING THE SURFACE

ADJECTIVE _____

NUMBER _____

ADJECTIVE _____

PART OF THE BODY (PLURAL) _____

PLURAL NOUN _____

NOUN _____

VERB ENDING IN "ING" _____

NOUN _____

ADJECTIVE _____

NOUN _____

ADJECTIVE _____

ADJECTIVE _____

PLURAL NOUN _____

MAD LIBS

VISITING THE SURFACE

One day, Leonardo asked Splinter a/an _Folty_ question.
ADJECTIVE

"We're _187_ years old! Isn't it time to let us explore the surface
NUMBER

world?" Master Splinter agreed, but only under the _Grumpy_
ADJECTIVE

condition that the Turtles not show their _Penis_ to
PART OF THE BODY (PLURAL)

anyone! Leonardo, Donatello, Raphael, and Michelangelo walked

through the sewer _Dorgeks_ and climbed up a/an
PLURAL NOUN

Shark. In the streets, car horns were _Funning_
NOUN   VERB ENDING IN "ING"

loudly. A boy went by slowly driving a white delivery _____.
NOUN

Raphael scared him off, but the boy left behind a flat box. Inside was a

hot, gooey, _____ circle. Was it food or a/an _____?
ADJECTIVE   NOUN

Mikey tried it. It was his first slice of pizza, and it was the most

_____ bite of food he had ever tasted. Then Donatello spotted
ADJECTIVE

a/an _____ teenage girl and her father, suddenly a van pulled
ADJECTIVE

up, and several strange men got out and threw the girl and her father

in the back of the van. The Turtles had to do something to stop these

_____, and fast!
PLURAL NOUN

MAD LIBS® is fun to play with friends, but you can also play it by yourself! To begin with, DO NOT look at the story on the page below. Fill in the blanks on this page with the words called for. Then, using the words you have selected, fill in the blank spaces in the story.

Now you've created your own hilarious MAD LIBS® game!

FIRST BATTLE WITH THE KRAANG

ADJECTIVE _____

ADJECTIVE _____

ADVERB _____

ADJECTIVE _____

VERB ENDING IN "ING" _____

PERSON IN ROOM (MALE) _____

ADVERB _____

PART OF THE BODY _____

NOUN _____

NOUN _____

NOUN _____

ADJECTIVE _____

EXCLAMATION _____

PART OF THE BODY _____

MAD LIBS

FIRST BATTLE WITH THE KRAANG

When we last left our ___colorful___ heroes, the Turtles were ready to
　　　　　　　　　　　ADJECTIVE

face a new enemy to save the man and girl in the van. Something

seemed ___scary___ about their enemy. They spoke ___kills___,
　　　　　ADJECTIVE　　　　　　　　　　　　　　　　　ADVERB

and they all looked the same. The Turtles were ___fire___ fighters,
　　　　　　　　　　　　　　　　　　　　　　　ADJECTIVE

but they were used to training by themselves. They didn't have much

practice _____ as a team, so they kept knocking into
　　　　　　VERB ENDING IN "ING"

one another and bumping shells. Donatello was about to free the girl

when out of nowhere _____ swung his nunchucks as
　　　　　　　　　　PERSON IN ROOM (MALE)

_____ as he could at Donnie. The nunchucks hit Donnie in the
ADVERB

_____, which gave him a lump the size of a/an _____.
PART OF THE BODY　　　　　　　　　　　　　　　　　　　　　NOUN

The van took off with the girl and her _____, and Leo, Raph,
　　　　　　　　　　　　　　　　　　　NOUN

and Donnie followed. Mikey stayed to face off against the one man

who was still standing. Mikey lashed out with his _____. The
　　　　　　　　　　　　　　　　　　　　　　　　NOUN

weapon hit the _____ man, and sparks flew everywhere.
　　　　　　　　ADJECTIVE

_____—sparks?! The man was a robot! And not just any
EXCLAMATION

robot, but a robot with a giant pink alien brain in its _____!
　　　　　　　　　　　　　　　　　　　　　　　　　　PART OF THE BODY

MAD LIBS® is fun to play with friends, but you can also play it by yourself! To begin with, DO NOT look at the story on the page below. Fill in the blanks on this page with the words called for. Then, using the words you have selected, fill in the blank spaces in the story.

Now you've created your own hilarious MAD LIBS® game!

I THINK HIS NAME IS BAXTER STOCKMAN

NOUN _____

NOUN _____

ADJECTIVE _____

ADJECTIVE _____

NOUN _____

PART OF THE BODY (PLURAL) _____

PERSON IN ROOM _____

PLURAL NOUN _____

ADJECTIVE _____

NOUN _____

ADJECTIVE _____

MAD LIBS®
I THINK HIS NAME IS BAXTER STOCKMAN

The Turtles were testing out Donatello's latest invention, a high-tech

portable music _____ called the T-Pod. While they were
                    NOUN

listening to the music on a rooftop, Raphael looked down into an alley

and spotted a villainous _____ wearing powered
                                NOUN

_____ armor. The Turtles ran down to the street and made
   ADJECTIVE

_____ work of him, then left him in a trash _____.
   ADJECTIVE   NOUN

When the Turtles returned home to the sewers, Michelangelo did not

have the _____ to tell the others that he had lost the
            PART OF THE BODY (PLURAL)

T-Pod in the fight. Later, Leonardo was watching *Space Heroes* on TV

when it cut to a news broadcast of the armored man, whose name was

_____ Stockman. He had been fired from his job and now he
 PERSON IN ROOM

wanted revenge! Baxter had the T-Pod, and it was powering his battle

_____. After a/an _____ fight, the Turtles were
  PLURAL NOUN   ADJECTIVE

finally able to throw a/an _____ filled with bees into Baxter's
                                NOUN

suit. While the bees distracted Baxter, Leonardo destroyed the T-Pod.

It was another _____ victory for the Turtles!
                    ADJECTIVE

MAD LIBS® is fun to play with friends, but you can also play it by yourself! To begin with, DO NOT look at the story on the page below. Fill in the blanks on this page with the words called for. Then, using the words you have selected, fill in the blank spaces in the story.

Now you've created your own hilarious MAD LIBS® game!

METALHEAD

ADJECTIVE _____

NOUN _____

PART OF THE BODY (PLURAL) _____

ADJECTIVE _____

NOUN _____

ADJECTIVE _____

ADVERB _____

EXCLAMATION _____

PLURAL NOUN _____

NUMBER _____

NOUN _____

NOUN _____

PLURAL NOUN _____

ADJECTIVE _____

MAD LIBS®

METALHEAD

Donatello never felt like he had an edge against the Kraang in their

_____ fights. That's because he only had a bo staff to fight
<u>ADJECTIVE</u>

with, which is a boring wooden _____. So he decided to use
<u>NOUN</u>

technology to fight the Kraang. He got his _____ on
<u>PART OF THE BODY (PLURAL)</u>

one of the busted Kraang robots, and transformed it into a/an

_____ robot turtle called Metalhead. At first, the other Turtles
<u>ADJECTIVE</u>

made fun of Donatello's metal _____, but then they saw how
<u>NOUN</u>

_____ the robo-turtle was in fights! But when he faced off
<u>ADJECTIVE</u>

against the Kraang, Metalhead stumbled around _____.
<u>ADVERB</u>

_____! Donatello hadn't worked out all the _____
<u>EXCLAMATION</u>   <u>PLURAL NOUN</u>

yet. After _____ minutes of fighting, the Kraang knocked
<u>NUMBER</u>

Metalhead onto the _____ and took control of him. The Kraang
<u>NOUN</u>

ordered _____-head to attack the Turtles! Master Splinter told
<u>NOUN</u>

Donatello that the only way he could save his _____ was to
<u>PLURAL NOUN</u>

join the fight himself, so Donatello raced to the scene, where he used

his _____ Turtle power to defeat Metalhead and the Kraang.
<u>ADJECTIVE</u>

MAD LIBS® is fun to play with friends, but you can also play it by yourself! To begin with, DO NOT look at the story on the page below. Fill in the blanks on this page with the words called for. Then, using the words you have selected, fill in the blank spaces in the story.

Now you've created your own hilarious MAD LIBS® game!

DOGPOUND AND FISHFACE HUNT THE TURTLES

ADJECTIVE _____

ADJECTIVE _____

PLURAL NOUN _____

ADVERB _____

VERB ENDING IN "ING" _____

NOUN _____

COLOR _____

ADJECTIVE _____

ANIMAL _____

NOUN _____

ADJECTIVE _____

MAD LIBS®

DOGPOUND AND FISHFACE HUNT THE TURTLES

The Shredder assigned his most _____ henchmen, Chris
                                   ADJECTIVE

Bradford and Xever, the task of defeating those _____ Ninja
                                                   ADJECTIVE

Turtles. Chris and Xever tried to set off a mutagen bomb that would

have turned every person in the city into _____, but the
                                              PLURAL NOUN

Turtles _____ defeated them. Chris said, "If I go down, I'm
          ADVERB

_____ you with me!" He stabbed the mutagen bomb
VERB ENDING IN "ING"

with his pointy _____. Mutagen soaked Chris and Xever and
                   NOUN

washed them away. Then the Shredder appeared to fight the Turtles

himself. The battle was interrupted when Chris and Xever returned.

They had been transformed by the Kraang mutagen. Chris had become

Dogpound, a giant _____ Akita. Xever had turned into a/an
                      COLOR

_____ flopping _____ called Fishface. To breathe
   ADJECTIVE   ANIMAL

and move on land, Fishface needed the help of Baxter Stockman, who

gave him cybernetic legs and a breathing _____. They may be
                                             NOUN

mutants, but Dogpound and Fishface want to defeat those

_____ Turtles more than anything!
   ADJECTIVE

MAD LIBS® is fun to play with friends, but you can also play it by yourself! To begin with, DO NOT look at the story on the page below. Fill in the blanks on this page with the words called for. Then, using the words you have selected, fill in the blank spaces in the story.

Now you've created your own hilarious MAD LIBS® game!

THE WEAPONS OF THE NINJA TURTLES

ADJECTIVE _____

ADJECTIVE _____

ANIMAL (PLURAL) _____

PLURAL NOUN _____

ADJECTIVE _____

ARTICLE OF CLOTHING _____

NUMBER _____

ADVERB _____

NOUN _____

PLURAL NOUN _____

PLURAL NOUN _____

ADVERB _____

MAD LIBS®
THE WEAPONS OF THE NINJA TURTLES

Many things make the Teenage Mutant Ninja Turtles _____
_____ ADJECTIVE

among heroes. For example, how many ninjas come with their own

_____ shells? But what makes the Ninja _____
ADJECTIVE   ANIMAL (PLURAL)

distinct from one another is their choice of weapons. There is no better

way to fight the Foot Clan and scary mutated _____ than
                                              PLURAL NOUN

with _____ ninja weapons. Leonardo, the gang's leader, who
     ADJECTIVE

wears a blue _____, uses not one but _____
             ARTICLE OF CLOTHING   NUMBER

katanas in battle. A katana is a razor-sharp sword that can _____
                                                            ADVERB

slice through any enemy. Donatello fights with a bo staff, which secretly

hides a piercing _____ at the end of the long stick. Raphael takes
                 NOUN

on enemies with his three-pronged sai, which are good at blocking

attacks from metal _____. Michelangelo swings his nunchucks,
                   PLURAL NOUN

which are two wooden _____ connected by a metal chain.
                     PLURAL NOUN

Sometimes Michelangelo uses a grappling hook to string up enemies.

But the truth is, the best weapon the Turtles have is teamwork. When

they work _____ as a team, no one can defeat them!
          ADVERB

MAD LIBS® is fun to play with friends, but you can also play it by yourself! To begin with, DO NOT look at the story on the page below. Fill in the blanks on this page with the words called for. Then, using the words you have selected, fill in the blank spaces in the story.

Now you've created your own hilarious MAD LIBS® game!

MOUSERS ATTACK!

ADJECTIVE _____

NOUN _____

PART OF THE BODY (PLURAL) _____

ADJECTIVE _____

NOUN _____

PERSON IN ROOM _____

VERB _____

PLURAL NOUN _____

ADVERB _____

PLURAL NOUN _____

ADJECTIVE _____

ADJECTIVE _____

NOUN _____

ADJECTIVE _____

MAD LIBS
MOUSERS ATTACK!

One _____ night in New York City, the Purple Dragons stole
      ADJECTIVE

April's _____. Leo and Raph investigated, but they found
         NOUN

themselves in over their _____ when the evil inventor
                    PART OF THE BODY (PLURAL)

Baxter Stockman attacked them with _____ robots called
                              ADJECTIVE

Mousers. Meanwhile, Donnie and Mikey tracked April's stolen

_____ to a factory where the giant mutant dog _____
   NOUN   PERSON IN ROOM

was plotting to _____ the Turtles. Donnie powered down the
            VERB

factory's _____, and the building went dark. Donnie and
         PLURAL NOUN

Mikey snuck in _____ but got caught by the bad guys, anyway.
            ADVERB

Leo and Raph hurried to rescue their captured _____, but
                                        PLURAL NOUN

Baxter's _____ Mousers were still on their tail. They freed
         ADJECTIVE

Donnie and Mikey, and then Donnie diverted the Mousers' attention

so the _____ Turtles could escape. Baxter was taken before
       ADJECTIVE

Shredder, who allowed Baxter to live because of his skills as a/an

_____. You'd have to be _____ not to accept a job
   NOUN   ADJECTIVE

offer from the Shredder!

MAD LIBS® is fun to play with friends, but you can also play it by yourself! To begin with, DO NOT look at the story on the page below. Fill in the blanks on this page with the words called for. Then, using the words you have selected, fill in the blank spaces in the story.

Now you've created your own hilarious MAD LIBS® game!

PROFILE: LEATHERHEAD

PLURAL NOUN _____

ADVERB _____

PLURAL NOUN _____

VERB ENDING IN "ING" _____

ADJECTIVE _____

ADJECTIVE _____

NOUN _____

A PLACE _____

ADJECTIVE _____

PLURAL NOUN _____

ADJECTIVE _____

ADJECTIVE _____

PART OF THE BODY (PLURAL) _____

PLURAL NOUN _____

MAD LIBS

PROFILE: LEATHERHEAD

Being an eight-foot-tall alligator is tough, especially when it comes to

finding _____ to be friends with. The Turtles suggested
         PLURAL NOUN

that I get _____ involved in social media. First, I tried the
          ADVERB

popular dating website, Love-_____.com. It goes without
                           PLURAL NOUN

_____ that it was not for me. Then Mikey said I
VERB ENDING IN "ING"

should create a/an _____ profile on MyFace.
                   ADJECTIVE

Name: Leatherhead, because my head is _____.
                                          ADJECTIVE

Favorite food: Pizza _____ soup.
                         NOUN

Interests: Tracking power cells in the sewers under (the) _____,
                                                             A PLACE

smashing Kraang with my _____ fists, and fixing up
                        ADJECTIVE

abandoned subway _____.
                 PLURAL NOUN

I don't think I'm going to have _____ luck finding friends
                               ADJECTIVE

with my profile. But now that I think about it, the Turtles have always

been _____ to me, even when I bash their
     ADJECTIVE

_____ in. I guess they are my true _____
PART OF THE BODY (PLURAL)   PLURAL NOUN

after all!

MAD LIBS® is fun to play with friends, but you can also play it by yourself! To begin with, DO NOT look at the story on the page below. Fill in the blanks on this page with the words called for. Then, using the words you have selected, fill in the blank spaces in the story.

Now you've created your own hilarious MAD LIBS® game!

THE TURTLES' FAVORITE PIZZA RECIPE

NOUN _____

A PLACE _____

PLURAL NOUN _____

NOUN _____

ADJECTIVE _____

COLOR _____

ANIMAL _____

NOUN _____

TYPE OF FOOD _____

NOUN _____

VERB _____

PLURAL NOUN _____

ADJECTIVE _____

MAD LIBS®
THE TURTLES' FAVORITE PIZZA RECIPE

Everyone knows that the Teenage Mutant Ninja Turtles love pizza. It's their favorite food. One day, the Turtles teamed up to make the best pizza in the history of the _____. First, Donatello ordered the

NOUN

dough from a classic Italian bakery in (the) _____. Raphael

A PLACE

made the tomato sauce with fresh vine-ripened _____, a

PLURAL NOUN

dash of red pepper flakes, and two sprigs of _____.

NOUN

Michelangelo used his own _____ recipe of four cheeses:

ADJECTIVE

mozzarella, parmesan, crumbles of _____ cheese, and

COLOR

Humboldt Fog, which is made from the milk of a/an _____.

ANIMAL

Leonardo sliced the pepperoni with his katana. He chopped up fruit

from a/an _____ tree, added two scoops of _____ ice

NOUN   TYPE OF FOOD

cream, and then topped the whole thing with spaghetti and

_____-balls. After the pizza had time to _____, the

NOUN   VERB

Turtles rolled it up like a taco and feasted like _____. They

PLURAL NOUN

offered some of their _____ pizza to Splinter, but he preferred

ADJECTIVE

to stick to sushi.

MAD LIBS® is fun to play with friends, but you can also play it by yourself! To begin with, DO NOT look at the story on the page below. Fill in the blanks on this page with the words called for. Then, using the words you have selected, fill in the blank spaces in the story.

Now you've created your own hilarious MAD LIBS® game!

RAT KING

PERSON IN ROOM _____

ADJECTIVE _____

NOUN _____

ANIMAL (PLURAL) _____

NOUN _____

ADVERB _____

NOUN _____

ADJECTIVE _____

ADJECTIVE _____

EXCLAMATION _____

ADVERB _____

PLURAL NOUN _____

Dr. _____ Falco was in his lasb trying to re-create his
\ PERSON IN ROOM

_____ neurochemical when his lab rats got loose, and
\ ADJECTIVE

set Dr. Falco's _____ on fire. Exposure to his
\ NOUN

neurochemical gave Dr. Falco the power to control the

_____ , and that's how he became the Rat King!
\ ANIMAL (PLURAL)

The Rat King set out to control Master Splinter, who was half rat, half

_____ . The Turtles tried to help their *sensei*, but Splinter
\ NOUN

was too powerful. Under the _____ defeated his pupils.
\ ADVERB

Leonardo tried to appeal to Splinter's human side, and showed him a

picture of his wife and _____ . At first, it looked like
\ NOUN

Splinter was still under the Rat King's _____ control—
\ ADJECTIVE

his eyes were _____ red. But then, _____ !
\ ADJECTIVE \ EXCLAMATION

It worked! Splinter broke the Rat King's control and fought back

_____ . After he found out he had lost Splinter, the Rat
\ ADVERB

King fled and disappeared in a swarm of _____ .
\ PLURAL NOUN

MAD LIBS® is fun to play with friends, but you can also play it by yourself! To begin with, DO NOT look at the story on the page below. Fill in the blanks on this page with the words called for. Then, using the words you have selected, fill in the blank spaces in the story.

Now you've created your own hilarious MAD LIBS® game!

NEW GIRL IN TOWN

ADJECTIVE _____

NOUN _____

NOUN _____

ADJECTIVE _____

NOUN _____

ADVERB _____

PART OF THE BODY _____

TYPE OF FOOD _____

ADJECTIVE _____

SAME PART OF THE BODY _____

PART OF THE BODY _____

ADJECTIVE _____

MAD LIBS

NEW GIRL IN TOWN

Leonardo and Raphael were arguing about the most _____
ADJECTIVE

way to catch the giant, mutated _____ Snakeweed. So Leo
NOUN

went off by himself, while Raph, Donnie, and Mikey chased Snakeweed

to an abandoned _____ factory. Leo encountered one of
NOUN

Shredder's _____ ninjas, but this one was different from the
ADJECTIVE

others. This ninja was a woman named Karai. She fought with a/an

_____, just like Leonardo. She seemed impressed with Leo's
NOUN

ninja skills. The two fighters were _____ matched. As a
ADVERB

member of the _____ Clan, Karai should have wanted to hurt
PART OF THE BODY

Leo. He didn't like her at all. But after she spared his life, Leo liked

Karai as much as Michelangelo liked _____ pizza! Leo went to
TYPE OF FOOD

April for advice. She was more than _____ to gossip about
ADJECTIVE

Karai. But when April found out that Karai was part of the

_____ Clan, she slapped Leo on the _____!
SAME PART OF THE BODY   PART OF THE BODY

Karai worked with the bad guys. But the most _____ surprise
ADJECTIVE

of all was that Karai calls Shredder "Father"!

MAD LIBS® is fun to play with friends, but you can also play it by yourself! To begin with, DO NOT look at the story on the page below. Fill in the blanks on this page with the words called for. Then, using the words you have selected, fill in the blank spaces in the story.

Now you've created your own hilarious MAD LIBS® game!

PERKS OF OWNING A SHELLRAISER

PLURAL NOUN _____

ADJECTIVE _____

ADVERB _____

PLURAL NOUN _____

VERB ENDING IN "ING" _____

NOUN _____

PLURAL NOUN _____

ADJECTIVE _____

ADJECTIVE _____

ADJECTIVE _____

TYPE OF FOOD _____

NOUN _____

ADJECTIVE _____

MAD LIBS®
PERKS OF OWNING
A SHELLRAISER

No one could have expected that an abandoned subway car covered in

_____ would one day be the Turtles' own _____
<u>PLURAL NOUN</u>   <u>ADJECTIVE</u>

transport, the Shellraiser. Donnie did most of the modifications

himself, building a/an _____ tubular combat vehicle. Foot
                        <u>ADVERB</u>

soldiers, gang members, and Kraang _____ alike quake at
                                    <u>PLURAL NOUN</u>

the sound of the Shellraiser's _____ engines. The
                                <u>VERB ENDING IN "ING"</u>

Shellraiser comes fully equipped with a garbage cannon, a manhole-

cover-flinging _____, and the most stylish paint job
                <u>NOUN</u>

_____ can buy. Each Turtle has his own _____
<u>PLURAL NOUN</u>   <u>ADJECTIVE</u>

duties aboard the Shellraiser. Leo drives, Mikey navigates, Raph

controls the _____ weapons, and Donnie has the most
              <u>ADJECTIVE</u>

_____ job of them all. He operates the Shellraiser's vital
<u>ADJECTIVE</u>

functions (but most importantly, the _____ oven)! Nothing
                                      <u>TYPE OF FOOD</u>

beats bulldozing Mousers into little pieces of _____ while
                                                <u>NOUN</u>

chowing down on a/an _____ slice of pizza.
                      <u>ADJECTIVE</u>

From TEENAGE MUTANT NINJA TURTLES MAD LIBS • © 2014 Viacom International Inc.
All Rights Reserved. Nickelodeon, Teenage Mutant Ninja Turtles, and all related titles, logos and characters are
trademarks of Viacom International Inc. Published by Price Stern Sloan, an imprint of Penguin Group (USA) LLC,
345 Hudson Street, New York, NY 10014.

MAD LIBS® is fun to play with friends, but you can also play it by yourself! To begin with, DO NOT look at the story on the page below. Fill in the blanks on this page with the words called for. Then, using the words you have selected, fill in the blank spaces in the story.

Now you've created your own hilarious MAD LIBS® game!

APRIL'S SECRET ADMIRER

ADJECTIVE _____

PLURAL NOUN _____

ADJECTIVE _____

PART OF THE BODY _____

NOUN _____

TYPE OF FOOD _____

VERB ENDING IN "ING" _____

ADJECTIVE _____

ADJECTIVE _____

ADJECTIVE _____

ARTICLE OF CLOTHING _____

PART OF THE BODY (PLURAL) _____

ADJECTIVE _____

PLURAL NOUN _____

ADJECTIVE _____

EXCLAMATION _____

NOUN _____

My dearest April,

From the moment I met you while you were getting attacked by

_____ _____, I have always thought you were
ADJECTIVE   PLURAL NOUN

the most _____ girl in the whole world. Your bright red
ADJECTIVE

_____ shimmers in the moonlight. Your cheeks are as fair as
PART OF THE BODY

a/an _____. Your eyes are as wide as a slice of _____.
NOUN   TYPE OF FOOD

I often wonder what it would be like to go out _____
VERB ENDING IN "ING"

together. But the _____ truth is, I can't tell you who I am. But
ADJECTIVE

I'll give you a few _____ hints. We've known each other for a
ADJECTIVE

while, and we are _____ friends. I wear a purple
ADJECTIVE

_____, and I have a gap between my two front
ARTICLE OF CLOTHING

_____. I have three brothers, and my skin is a/an
PART OF THE BODY (PLURAL)

_____ green color. People say I'm good at fixing
ADJECTIVE

_____ and designing _____ new technologies! If
PLURAL NOUN   ADJECTIVE

you ever need a study buddy, or a boyfriend, then I'm your Turtle.

_____! I mean I'm your _____.
EXCLAMATION   NOUN

MAD LIBS® is fun to play with friends, but you can also play it by yourself! To begin with, DO NOT look at the story on the page below. Fill in the blanks on this page with the words called for. Then, using the words you have selected, fill in the blank spaces in the story.

Now you've created your own hilarious MAD LIBS® game!

VACATIONING IN DIMENSION X

ADJECTIVE _____

PLURAL NOUN _____

NOUN _____

NOUN _____

ADJECTIVE _____

NUMBER _____

NOUN _____

PART OF THE BODY _____

ADJECTIVE _____

PLURAL NOUN _____

VERB ENDING IN "ING" _____

ADJECTIVE _____

ADJECTIVE _____

MAD LIBS®
VACATIONING IN DIMENSION X

After a long, _____ day at the office filing _____
          ADJECTIVE   PLURAL NOUN

and gossiping with friends at the _____ cooler, don't you feel
                                            NOUN

like you need a vacation? If so, then I have the travel destination for

you and your _____. It's Dimension X! Homeworld of the
                         NOUN

_____ alien race the Kraang, and the multiverse's number
  ADJECTIVE

_____ hottest vacation spot. Surf's up on the oceans of molten
  NUMBER

_____ just outside your hotel. If athletics is more your style,
  NOUN

try your _____ at gladiator combat in Dimension X's largest
      PART OF THE BODY

arena. What vacation would be complete without a visit with the

_____ local population? Yes, in Dimension X, you will have
  ADJECTIVE

the chance to converse with the lovable _____, the Kraang,
                                       PLURAL NOUN

the _____ brains with faces. Sure, to get to Dimension
    VERB ENDING IN "ING"

X, you'll need a/an _____ teleporter, which can be really
                ADJECTIVE

expensive, but don't worry—the Kraang are doing everything they can

to make Earth more like their _____ home. You might be
                           ADJECTIVE

visiting Dimension X soon, whether you want to or not!

MAD LIBS® is fun to play with friends, but you can also play it by yourself! To begin with, DO NOT look at the story on the page below. Fill in the blanks on this page with the words called for. Then, using the words you have selected, fill in the blank spaces in the story.

Now you've created your own hilarious MAD LIBS® game!

THE PULVERIZER

PLURAL NOUN _____

ADJECTIVE _____

PLURAL NOUN _____

ADJECTIVE _____

NOUN _____

PLURAL NOUN _____

ADJECTIVE _____

VERB ENDING IN "ING" _____

PLURAL NOUN _____

ADJECTIVE _____

ADJECTIVE _____

VERB _____

NOUN _____

MAD LIBS

THE PULVERIZER

The Teenage Mutant Ninja _____ were tracking a group of
                          PLURAL NOUN

Purple Dragons in the Shellraiser when they encountered a/an

_____ man dressed up like Raphael. His name was the
   ADJECTIVE

Pulverizer, and he was going to pulverize the Purple _____.
                                                      PLURAL NOUN

The Pulverizer was a/an _____ fan of the Turtles, but he didn't
                          ADJECTIVE

know the first _____ about ninjutsu. Donatello tried to teach
                  NOUN

him some ninja _____, but the Pulverizer proved to be
                 PLURAL NOUN

_____. Later, the Turtles were _____ with a
   ADJECTIVE   VERB ENDING IN "ING"

team of Foot Soldiers, only to discover that the clumsiest of the

_____ was actually the Pulverizer! "Shredder must really be
   PLURAL NOUN

_____ to recruit him!" Raphael said. The Pulverizer told the
   ADJECTIVE

Turtles he had a/an _____ idea. He could be a spy that could
                       ADJECTIVE

_____ on Shredder and the Foot Clan. The Turtles were
   VERB

worried. They needed a spy like the Pulverizer like a fish needs a/an

_____!
    NOUN

MAD LIBS® is fun to play with friends, but you can also play it by yourself! To begin with, DO NOT look at the story on the page below. Fill in the blanks on this page with the words called for. Then, using the words you have selected, fill in the blank spaces in the story.

Now you've created your own hilarious MAD LIBS® game!

SPECIAL DELIVERY: MUTAGEN!

PERSON IN ROOM _____

VERB _____

NOUN _____

ADJECTIVE _____

PLURAL NOUN _____

VERB ENDING IN "ING" _____

ADJECTIVE _____

PART OF THE BODY _____

PART OF THE BODY (PLURAL) _____

ADVERB _____

ADJECTIVE _____

A PLACE _____

NOUN _____

ADVERB _____

VERB ENDING IN "ING" _____

NOUN _____

MAD LIBS
SPECIAL DELIVERY:
MUTAGEN!

One Saturday morning, you and your best friend _____ are
PERSON IN ROOM

about to _____ in front of the TV when you hear a deafening
VERB

_____. A/An _____ alien spaceship is flying over
NOUN ADJECTIVE

your house, dropping _____ filled with mutagen! You race
PLURAL NOUN

outside. People are _____ around the neighborhood,
VERB ENDING IN "ING"

covered in mutagen. One of the _____ globs of mutagen lands
ADJECTIVE

on your friend's _____, just as your neighbor's dog runs past
PART OF THE BODY

you. Then your friend mutates before your _____
PART OF THE BODY (PLURAL)

into a giant dog! You race _____ to school, which looks like it
ADVERB

has been taken over by monsters. But the monsters are actually just

your teachers, who have mutated into _____ hamsters and
ADJECTIVE

iguanas. Class is canceled, so you head back to (the) _____.
A PLACE

But on the way, an enormous glob of _____ falls out of the
NOUN

sky and covers you _____. Your fingers tingle and your toes
ADVERB

tickle. You feel yourself _____. In an instant, you've
VERB ENDING IN "ING"

become a giant _____!
NOUN

From TEENAGE MUTANT NINJA TURTLES MAD LIBS • © 2014 Viacom International Inc.
All Rights Reserved. Nickelodeon, Teenage Mutant Ninja Turtles, and all related titles, logos and characters are
trademarks of Viacom International Inc. Published by Price Stern Sloan, an imprint of Penguin Group (USA) LLC,
345 Hudson Street, New York, NY 10014.

MAD LIBS® is fun to play with friends, but you can also play it by yourself! To begin with, DO NOT look at the story on the page below. Fill in the blanks on this page with the words called for. Then, using the words you have selected, fill in the blank spaces in the story.

Now you've created your own hilarious MAD LIBS® game!

OPERATION: BREAKOUT

A PLACE _____

ADJECTIVE _____

NOUN _____

ANIMAL _____

NOUN _____

PART OF THE BODY _____

PART OF THE BODY _____

ADJECTIVE _____

PLURAL NOUN _____

ADJECTIVE _____

ADJECTIVE _____

VERB ENDING IN "ING" _____

NOUN _____

MA☺IBS

OPERATION: BREAKOUT

One day while the Turtles were sparring in (the) _____, April
                                                 A PLACE
received a message. It was a distress call from April's father, who was

still a captive of the _____ aliens, the Kraang. Donnie wanted
                        ADJECTIVE
to impress April so he went to the Kraang lab by himself to rescue Mr.

O'Neil. Donnie found April's dad, but got into deep _____
                                                          NOUN
when a giant mutant _____ and the Kraang discovered him.
                      ANIMAL
The other Turtles arrived in the nick of _____, and they all
                                            NOUN
escaped. Unfortunately, they didn't notice that someone had planted a

mind _____ control device on the back of Mr. O'Neil's
      PART OF THE BODY
_____, which meant he was being controlled by the
PART OF THE BODY
_____ Shredder. April's dad tricked his daughter into being
 ADJECTIVE
captured by Karai and her band of masked ninja _____. At
                                                   PLURAL NOUN
the same time, the Kraang had initiated the final phase of their

_____ plan to take over planet Earth. The Turtles took the
 ADJECTIVE
battle to the Kraang's _____ _____ death
                          ADJECTIVE   VERB ENDING IN "ING"
_____—the Technodrome!
 NOUN

MAD LIBS® is fun to play with friends, but you can also play it by yourself! To begin with, DO NOT look at the story on the page below. Fill in the blanks on this page with the words called for. Then, using the words you have selected, fill in the blank spaces in the story.

Now you've created your own hilarious MAD LIBS® game!

A TRAGIC HISTORY

VERB _____

ADJECTIVE _____

PLURAL NOUN _____

PART OF THE BODY _____

ADJECTIVE _____

ADVERB _____

A PLACE _____

NOUN _____

ADVERB _____

VERB (PAST TENSE) _____

PLURAL NOUN _____

ADJECTIVE _____

ADJECTIVE _____

MAD☺IBS

A TRAGIC HISTORY

Nothing could _____ in Splinter's way as he went to confront
<u>VERB</u>

his old rival, the Shredder. He wiped out a squad of Shredder's

_____ ninja _____ with ease. Then he faced
<u>ADJECTIVE</u>   <u>PLURAL NOUN</u>

Dogpound and Fish-_____. Splinter used his ninjutsu to
<u>PART OF THE BODY</u>

make the two _____ mutants crash into each other. After
<u>ADJECTIVE</u>

Splinter defeated them _____, he faced the Shredder. The last
<u>ADVERB</u>

time they met was years ago, in (the) _____, Japan. Splinter
<u>A PLACE</u>

said that he had considered Shredder his brother and a member of his

own _____. But Oroku Saki was _____ jealous of
<u>NOUN</u>   <u>ADVERB</u>

Splinter, so he started a fire that _____ Splinter's wife.
<u>VERB (PAST TENSE)</u>

Then Shredder stole Splinter's daughter, Miwa. That's right. Karai is

Miwa! But Karai didn't know heads from _____ about any
<u>PLURAL NOUN</u>

of this. Karai attacked Splinter, but he could not fight his own

_____ daughter. He returned to the sewers, dejected and
<u>ADJECTIVE</u>

_____.
<u>ADJECTIVE</u>

MAD LIBS® is fun to play with friends, but you can also play it by yourself! To begin with, DO NOT look at the story on the page below. Fill in the blanks on this page with the words called for. Then, using the words you have selected, fill in the blank spaces in the story.

Now you've created your own hilarious MAD LIBS® game!

BOOYAKA-SHOWDOWN!

EXCLAMATION _____

NOUN _____

ADJECTIVE _____

NOUN _____

NOUN _____

TYPE OF FOOD _____

ADJECTIVE _____

ADJECTIVE _____

PLURAL NOUN _____

ADJECTIVE _____

NOUN _____

NOUN _____

ADJECTIVE _____

ADVERB _____

MAD☺LIBS®
BOOYAKA-SHOWDOWN!

_____! The Turtles had infiltrated the Technodrome to rescue
EXCLAMATION

their _____ April and stop the Kraang once and for all.
NOUN

Donatello set April free, and the Turtles fought a/an _____
ADJECTIVE

battle and defeated Kraang Prime. But the alien overlord wasn't done

yet. As the Turtles tried to escape with April, Kraang Prime emerged in

a massive robotic suit that made the alien look as tall as a/an

_____. Leo stayed on board the _____ to fight
NOUN   NOUN

Kraang Prime while the other Turtles escaped with April. When the

Technodrome crashed into the ocean, Raphael thought Leo was

_____. He was so _____! Raph apologized to Leo
TYPE OF FOOD   ADJECTIVE

and wished he had been nice instead of _____. But then the
ADJECTIVE

Turtles heard loud _____ as Leo surged out of the ocean in
PLURAL NOUN

a spray of water. He was alive! The Turtles and April returned to their

sewer lair, where, with _____ dance moves, the Turtles cut a/
ADJECTIVE

an _____, grooved, ate lots of _____ and
NOUN   NOUN

_____ olive pizza, and partied _____ until dawn.
ADJECTIVE   ADVERB